D1203759

BIOGRAPHIES *of the*
NEW WORLD POWER
RUTHERFORD B. HAYES, THOMAS ALVA EDISON, MARGARET SANGER, AND MORE

BIOGRAPHIES *of the*
NEW WORLD POWER

RUTHERFORD B. HAYES, THOMAS ALVA EDISON, MARGARET SANGER, AND MORE

Edited by Michael Anderson

Britannica®
Educational Publishing
IN ASSOCIATION WITH

ROSEN
EDUCATIONAL SERVICES

Published in 2013 by Britannica Educational Publishing
(a trademark of Encyclopædia Britannica, Inc.)
in association with Rosen Educational Services, LLC
29 East 21st Street, New York, NY 10010.

First Edition

Britannica Educational Publishing
J.E. Luebering: Director, Core Reference Group, Encyclopædia Britannica
Adam Augustyn: Assistant Manager, Encyclopædia Britannica

Anthony L. Green: Editor, Compton's by Britannica
Michael Anderson: Senior Editor, Compton's by Britannica
Andrea R. Field: Senior Editor, Compton's by Britannica
Sherman Hollar: Associate Editor, Compton's by Britannica

Marilyn L. Barton: Senior Coordinator, Production Control
Steven Bosco: Director, Editorial Technologies
Lisa S. Braucher: Senior Producer and Data Editor
Yvette Charboneau: Senior Copy Editor
Kathy Nakamura: Manager, Media Acquisition

Rosen Educational Services
Nicholas Croce: Editor
Nelson Sá: Art Director
Cindy Reiman: Photography Manager
Karen Huang: Photo Researcher
Brian Garvey: Designer, Cover Design
Introduction by Nicholas Croce

Library of Congress Cataloging-in-Publication Data

Biographies of the new world power: Rutherford B. Hayes, Thomas Alva Edison, Margaret Sanger,
and more/edited by Michael Anderson.
       p. cm.—(Impact on America: collective biographies)
"In association with Britannica Educational Publishing, Rosen Educational Services."
Includes bibliographical references and index.
ISBN 978-1-61530-691-6 (library binding)
1. United States—Biography—Juvenile literature. 2. United States—History—1865-1898—Juvenile
literature. 3. United States—History—20th century—Juvenile literature. I. Anderson, Michael, 1972–
E663.B63 2012
920.073—dc23

                                                                              2012001226

Manufactured in the United States of America

Cover, p. 3 © iStockphoto.com/kledge (flag), Library of Congress Prints and Photographs Division
(Rutherford B. Hayes, Margaret Sanger)

Interior background © www.istockphoto.com/oliopi (geometric), © www.istockphoto.com/Bill Noll
(floral)

Back cover © www.istockphoto.com/Sodafish bvba

20

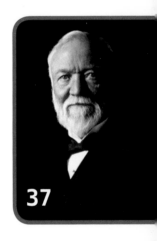

37

55

99

103

136

INTRODUCTION

The era explored in this collection of biographies—the late 19th and early 20th centuries—represents the maturation of the United States into a world power. Moving on from the divisions that plagued the nation during the Civil War and Reconstruction, the United States transformed itself politically, economically, culturally, and socially. Many of these changes are embodied in the lives of the figures profiled here.

Marking the beginning of this era was the decision by President Rutherford B. Hayes to remove the last federal troops from the South in 1877, ending the bitter Reconstruction period. Under the leadership of the 25th president, William McKinley, the United States extended its influence overseas by making territorial acquisitions following the Spanish-American War in 1898. Following McKinley, President Theodore Roosevelt continued the momentum of American internationalism by using what he called the "bully pulpit" of the presidency to promote the nation's role and responsibilities in politics beyond its borders. "Speak softly and carry a big stick," Roosevelt said of his policy on relations with other countries, which displayed the new maturity and resolve of the nation.

Yet, with its expanding influence and growing fortunes, the United States suffered from new economic disparities. John D. Rockefeller, Andrew Carnegie, and Jay Gould amassed great dynastic wealth from oil, steel, and railroads, respectively, and other industrialists and financiers found similar success, often at the expense of workers. Because of their fortunes and the growing gap between rich and poor, Roosevelt would later brand these capitalists "malefactors of great wealth," inspiring a new age of activism for the lower classes. Labor leaders, social workers, novelists, and journalists such as Samuel Gompers, Jane Addams, Upton Sinclair, and Jacob Riis shone a light on the plight of the poor, figuratively and, in the case of Riis's photography, literally. Using the newly invented flashbulb, Riis photographed the New York slums of the late 19th century, exposing the city and the nation to shocking scenes of poverty existing alongside such great fortune.

While these activists advocated for the economically disadvantaged, others took up the causes of historically oppressed groups. Women's rights advocates such as Margaret Sanger and Susan B. Anthony gave women a voice on issues such as birth control and suffrage. African Americans were championed by the journalist Ida B. Wells-Barnett, who spearheaded an antilynching campaign and other initiatives aimed at racial justice. And in 1909, just 46 years after the Emancipation Proclamation, the African American editor, historian, and sociologist W. E. B Du Bois helped found the National Association for the Advancement of Colored People (NAACP). Another individual who contributed to the discussion of race in the United States was Mark Twain, whose classic and controversial novel *Huckleberry Finn* addressed the shameful legacy of slavery in the antebellum South and the persistent racial discrimination and violence.

After the end of the Reconstruction period, the United States began to grow into a world power of unprecedented wealth and

cultural and social awareness. It would continue to build power and prestige until, by
the end of World War II, it was the strongest
nation in the world. The social reform movements that took root in the late 19th and
early 20th centuries also would endure, with
the strengthening of the labor movement
and the reemergence of the civil rights and
women's movements in the 1960s and '70s.
The individuals profiled in this volume are
just a sample of the great leaders who helped
shape the nation during this formative period
of American history.

The presidential election of 1876 between Rutherford B. Hayes and Samuel Tilden was among the most bitterly contested in U.S. history. Both the Democrats and the Republicans accused each other of fraud. Not until March 2, two days before Pres. Ulysses S. Grant's term expired, was the issue at last settled. The electoral commission decided in favor of the Republican candidate, Hayes. After eight years of corruption in Washington, Hayes tried to establish new standards of integrity in the White House.

EARLY LIFE AND CAREER

Rutherford Birchard Hayes was born in Delaware, Ohio, on Oct. 4, 1822. At 16 he entered Kenyon College in Gambier, Ohio, and in 1842 he graduated at the head of his class. He then attended Harvard Law School in Cambridge, Mass., receiving a bachelor of laws degree in 1845. Returning to Ohio, he established a successful legal practice in Cincinnati.

Hayes also entered local politics in the new Republican party. While serving in the Union Army during the American Civil War, he was nominated and elected to the U.S. Congress. He took his seat in the House of Representatives in December 1865 and was reelected in 1866. He then served three terms as governor of Ohio, attracting national attention with his strong advocacy of a sound currency backed by gold.

THE DISPUTED PRESIDENTIAL ELECTION

The Republican nominating convention for the 1876 presidential election met in Cincinnati. The leading candidate, Senator James G. Blaine of Maine, had been accused of graft, and reformers controlled the convention. Hayes, Ohio's "favorite son," won the nomination. The Democratic party also nominated a reform candidate, Samuel J. Tilden. The campaign was bitterly fought, though the platforms of the two major parties differed little. Tilden won a popular majority, and early returns indicated a Democratic victory in the electoral college as well.

On election night Hayes went to bed convinced that he had lost. The next day, however, his campaign managers challenged the legitimacy of the returns from South Carolina, Florida, and Louisiana, and as a result two sets of ballots were submitted from the three states. Congress debated the election for weeks. The Senate, which was Republican, declared for Hayes. The House, which was Democratic, said Tilden had won. Finally Congress appointed an electoral commission to re-count the entire vote. The commission consisted of eight Republicans and seven Democrats. The vote on every count was eight to seven.

When it became clear that the commission would decide for Hayes, the Southern Democrats agreed to accept him if the Republicans would enter into a "bargain." More than the election of Tilden, they wanted federal troops withdrawn from the South and the return of self-government to the states. The Republicans agreed, and on March 2 the commission announced that Hayes had 185 electoral votes and Tilden 184. The result was greeted with outrage by some Northern Democrats, who thereafter referred to Hayes as His Fraudulency.

PRESIDENCY

The presidency was weak and Congress strong when Hayes moved into the White House. Powerful senators had impeached President Andrew Johnson and subdued Grant. They expected to control Hayes also and were by no means pleased with the tone of his inaugural address. The people of the country, however, applauded his much-quoted statement, "He serves his party best who serves his country best."

Hayes incurred the enmity of many Republican leaders by carrying out the "bargain." The Southern Republican governments to which Hayes owed his election collapsed, and the South thereafter became solidly Democratic. In April 1877 the last federal troops were withdrawn from the South, and the long, bitter period of Reconstruction was at last ended.

Hayes's policies toward the South angered conservative Republicans known as the Stalwarts. The president further offended this group with his efforts to end the corrupt "spoils system"—the giving of government jobs to party workers as a reward for securing votes. The worst abuses of the spoils system

were in the customhouse of New York City. Hayes ignited a bitter dispute with Senator Roscoe Conkling of New York by dismissing Conkling's political friends from the top posts. One of the officials he dismissed was Chester A. Arthur, who was later to become the 21st president of the United States.

Another achievement of Hayes's term was the return to a stable paper currency backed by gold. This meant that every paper dollar the federal government printed was matched by a gold dollar that the government kept in reserve. This increased the public's confidence in the money supply. Hayes's "hard money" policy helped pull the country out of its economic depression. When Hayes left the White House the country was again prosperous.

RETIREMENT

Hayes had said before his election that he would not be a candidate for a second term. Back in Fremont, Ohio, he devoted himself to humanitarian causes, working for prison reform and for improved education and training for blacks in the South. He died in Fremont on Jan. 17, 1893.

CHAPTER 2

When he was 21 years old, Thomas Edison took out his first patent. It was for an electric vote counter to be used in the U.S. House of Representatives. The machine worked perfectly, but the congressmen would not buy it. They did not want vote counting to be done quickly. Often the roll call was used for purposes of delay (filibustering).

This experience taught the young inventor a lesson. He decided to follow a simple rule: "First, be sure a thing is wanted or needed, then go ahead." By the time he died at 84, Edison had patented, singly or jointly, 1,093 inventions. Many were among the most useful and helpful inventions ever developed—including the motion-picture camera, the phonograph, and the incandescent electric lightbulb.

EARLY LIFE AND CAREER

Thomas Alva Edison was born in Milan, Ohio, on Feb. 11, 1847. When he was seven, he moved with his family to Port Huron, Mich. There he went to school for a few months—the only formal schooling he ever had. He was educated mostly at home by his mother. By the time he was 12, he had also begun to do chemistry experiments and had his own laboratory in his father's basement.

When he was 13, Edison began working on the Grand Trunk Railroad between Port Huron and Detroit, selling newspapers and candy. To continue his chemistry experiments he set up a laboratory in a baggage car on the train. He also began publishing his own newspaper there on a press that had been used for printing handbills.

At about this time Edison lost almost all of his hearing. A number of explanations have been given for his deafness. One story, told by Edison himself, is that a conductor once took him by both ears to lift him onto the train. Edison felt something snap in his head, and his deafness began then. It is more likely that his hearing problems were due to a type of infection that ran in his family.

When Edison was 15, he saved the life of a child who was playing in the path of an oncoming train. The boy's grateful father offered to teach Edison how to be a telegraph operator. He soon learned Morse code and became skilled in sending and taking messages. From 1863 to 1868 he worked as a telegrapher, but he was more interested in working on his own inventions. Soon he had made enough progress with a duplex telegraph (a device capable of sending two messages simultaneously on one wire) and a printing telegraph that he decided to become a full-time inventor.

Edison moved to New York, where he developed a stock printer and other printing telegraphs. He used the money he earned to start a laboratory and factory in Newark, N.J. He soon had 300 employees and began turning out a number of successful inventions, most having to do with telegraphy.

MENLO PARK

After five years in Newark, Edison opened a new laboratory and machine shop in Menlo Park, N.J. There, from 1876 to 1886, he did his finest work. He soon became world famous as the Wizard of Menlo Park.

Edison's success was due in part to his work habits. In the picture above the inventor appears somewhat haggard at the close of five days and five nights of continuous work in perfecting the early wax-cylinder type of phonograph. **U.S. Department of the Interior, National Park Service, Edison National Historic Site**

Edison's early work at Menlo Park centered on the telephone, which had been introduced by Alexander Graham Bell in 1876. The first Bell telephone was both a transmitter and a receiver. One spoke through it and then put it to one's ear to hear the reply. The instrument was also weak in reproducing the voice and picked up much static. Edison invented a carbon transmitter that greatly improved the telephone's sound capabilities. It was the standard design in telephone transmitters until the 1970s.

Edison's telephone work led to his invention in 1877 of the first device that could record and reproduce sound—the phonograph. He called it a "talking machine." When Edison first demonstrated the machine to his laboratory assistants, they were startled to hear the inventor's voice coming from it. For a time they thought Edison was playing a trick on them. Later, when everyone had become convinced of the reality of Edison's invention, he became world famous.

Edison next focused his efforts on producing an electric light to replace gas lighting. Although electric lighting had existed since the early 19th century, it was not yet practical for home use. Edison's aim was to invent

21

a lamp that would become incandescent, or luminous, as a result of heat passing through it. After many months of work, Edison introduced the first commercially practical incandescent electric light in 1879.

Edison also devoted his energies to improving the dynamo to furnish the necessary power for electric lighting systems. In addition, he developed a complete system of distributing the current and built the first central power station in lower Manhattan in 1882.

"INVENTION FACTORY" IN WEST ORANGE

In 1887 Edison opened a new laboratory in West Orange, N.J. He called it his "invention factory." The first major undertaking at the new laboratory was a return to the phonograph, which Edison had abandoned to work on electric lighting. Spurred by the work of competitors, including Alexander Graham Bell, Edison worked to create a phonograph that was practical for business and home use. In the 1890s he established facilities for the production of both phonographs and the records to play on them.

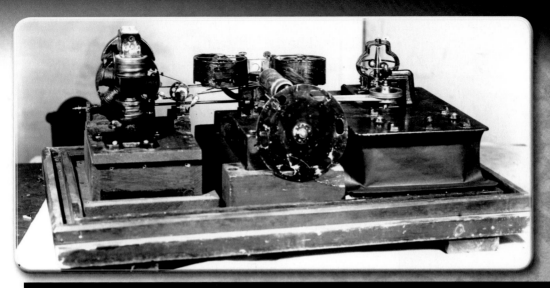

The Kinetograph was an early motion-picture camera developed by Thomas A. Edison and William Dickson by 1890. **U.S. Department of the Interior, National Park Service, Edison National Historic Site**

Meanwhile, in 1888, Edison and William K.L. Dickson had developed a motion-picture camera and a projector. The camera was called the Kinetograph. The projector, called the Kinetoscope, was a small box inside which the motion picture was projected. The picture was viewed through a peephole, meaning that only one person at a time could view the show. Competitors soon developed projectors that displayed the pictures on a screen.

Another important product of the West Orange laboratory was the alkaline storage

battery. By 1909, after a decade of work on the project, Edison was a principal supplier of batteries for submarines and electric vehicles and had even formed a company for the manufacture of electric automobiles.

LATER YEARS

Although his later projects were not as successful as his earlier ones, Edison continued to work even in his 80s. He died in West Orange on Oct. 18, 1931. His West Orange laboratory and his 23-room home, Glenmont, were designated a national historic site in 1955.

When President James A. Garfield was assassinated in 1881, Chester A. Arthur, the vice president, rose to the highest office of the United States. Arthur took the presidential oath on Sept. 19, 1881, amid widespread belief that he was unworthy of the office. Said to be hurt by the public's low regard for him, Arthur was determined to prove that he could rise above expectations.

EARLY LIFE AND LAW PRACTICE

Chester Alan Arthur was born in Fairfield, Vt., on Oct. 5, 1829. His parents were William Arthur, a Baptist minister, and Malvina Stone Arthur. In 1844, when he was only 15, Arthur was admitted to Union College in Schenectady, N.Y. To support himself financially, he began to teach during the long winter vacations. After graduating at 18, he continued to teach while studying law.

William Arthur was an abolitionist, and his son shared his views on slavery. In the

Chester A. Arthur. **SuperStock/Getty Images**

minister's congregation was a congressman, Erastus D. Culver, who also had strong anti-slavery principles. Culver moved his law office to Brooklyn and agreed to take Arthur into his firm to train him. Arthur entered Culver's office in 1853 and was admitted to the bar a year later.

Arthur arrived in time to assist Culver in the famous Lemmon slave case. In 1852 Jonathan Lemmon and his wife had brought eight slaves from Virginia to New York by boat. They intended to stop over only until the next boat left for Texas. The court decided that slaves passing through New York became free.

Meanwhile Arthur was fighting another civil rights case. An African American woman, Lizzie Jennings, had been forced off a Brooklyn streetcar by the conductor and some of the passengers. Arthur won damages of $500 for her and, more importantly, obtained a court decision forbidding discrimination in public transportation.

POLITICAL CAREER

Arthur played an important part in the organization of the new Republican party in the

state of New York, but he was never interested in holding political office. During the Civil War he served as quartermaster general of New York's troops. The post involved supplying barracks, food, uniforms, and equipment for the troops who passed through the city.

Arthur resumed his law practice in 1863. His political activities brought him into close association with Senator Roscoe Conkling, the Republican boss of New York. In 1871, with Conkling's backing, Arthur was appointed customs collector of the port of New York by President Ulysses S. Grant. The New York Custom House, which collected about two thirds of the country's tariff revenue, was known for flagrant use of the spoils system, by which Conkling's political supporters were rewarded with government jobs. Arthur collected customs duties with integrity, but he was not a reformer. When an appointment was to be made, he looked for a qualified political friend to do the work.

Civil-service reform was in full swing when Rutherford B. Hayes succeeded Grant as president in 1877. Hayes decided to organize the New York Custom House on a strictly business basis. In 1878 he suspended Arthur, who returned to his law practice.

The Republican party was seriously divided in 1880. Conkling, as leader of the Stalwart Republicans, tried to nominate Grant for a third term. The "Half-Breed" (moderate) Republicans wanted Senator James G. Blaine. The deadlock in the convention lasted until the 36th ballot, when James A. Garfield was unexpectedly nominated as a compromise candidate. To make sure of the Stalwarts' aid in the election, the convention nominated Arthur for vice president. The Republicans won the election and Arthur took the country's second highest office.

PRESIDENCY

On July 2, 1881, Garfield was shot by a disappointed office seeker who boasted that he was a Stalwart Republican. During the weeks when Garfield lingered between life and death, popular indignation against the Stalwarts ran high. Arthur remained in seclusion until Garfield's death in September made him president. The public considered the former customhouse collector unqualified for the office.

In his first message to Congress, Arthur surprised everyone by coming out strongly

for civil-service reform. In 1883 he signed the country's first civil-service law, the Pendleton Act. This act set up a civil-service commission to conduct competitive examinations for people seeking government jobs. It was the first important step toward replacing the spoils system with a merit-based system for filling government offices.

Arthur is called the Father of the American Navy because he took a personal interest in modernizing and expanding it. The Navy had declined steadily after the Civil War. In 1882 Congress appropriated money for the country's first all-steel vessels. The so-called "white squadron" formed the nucleus of the modern U.S. Navy.

Arthur's popularity grew with each year of his presidency. In 1884 he hoped to receive approval from the Republican nominating convention, but he was not seriously considered. Despondent, Arthur returned to his New York home and tried to resume his law practice, but he lacked the energy for it. He died on Nov. 18, 1886.

The late 19th century in the United States was the era of "robber baron" capitalists, those whom Theodore Roosevelt called "malefactors of great wealth." Jay Gould was one of the shrewdest and most successful. As a financier he was totally unscrupulous. Through stock swindles and speculation he reaped millions in profits, but at the end of his life he was alone and friendless.

Jason Gould was born on May 27, 1836, in Roxbury, N.Y. He grew up in poverty and had little schooling. By 1857 he had earned enough money to open a tannery in Pennsylvania, and three years later he began speculating in railroad stocks. By 1867 he was a director of the Erie Railroad. By selling the public shares in the railroad for much more money than it was worth, he and his fellow directors earned millions; by looting the railroad of its assets, they earned more. He and associate James Fisk were involved in a gold speculation scheme that led to Black Friday—Sept. 24, 1869—when

a financial panic was caused by a sudden fall in the price of gold. The speculators had entangled President Ulysses S. Grant in their plot, and his reputation suffered when the panic hit.

In 1872 Gould was forced out of Erie, and he went on to control western railroads, the Western Union Telegraph Company, and New York City's elevated railway system. At one time he owned half the railroad right of way in the Southwest. From 1879 to 1883 he owned the *New York World* newspaper. He associated with some of the most corrupt politicians of his time, including the notorious William Marcy "Boss" Tweed of New York. Gould worked at his financial schemes until nearly the end of his life. He died in New York City on Dec. 2, 1892.

CHAPTER 5

JOHN D. ROCKEFELLER

An industrialist and philanthropist, John D. Rockefeller founded the Standard Oil Company. The company dominated the oil industry and was the first great U.S. business trust.

John Davison Rockefeller was born on July 8, 1839, in Richford, N.Y. He moved with his family to Cleveland, Ohio, in 1853, and six years later he established his first enterprise—a commission business dealing in hay, grain, meats, and other goods. Sensing the commercial potential of the expanding oil production in western Pennsylvania in the early 1860s, he built his first oil refinery, near Cleveland, in 1863. Within two years it was the largest refinery in the area, and thereafter Rockefeller devoted himself exclusively to the oil business.

In 1870 Rockefeller and a few associates incorporated the Standard Oil Company (Ohio). Because of Rockefeller's emphasis on economical operations, Standard prospered and began to buy out its competitors until, by 1872, it controlled nearly all the refineries in Cleveland. That fact enabled the company to negotiate with railroads for favored rates on its shipments of oil. It acquired pipelines and terminal facilities, purchased competing refineries in other cities, and vigorously sought to expand its markets in the United States and abroad. By 1882 it had a near monopoly of the oil business in the United States. In 1881 Rockefeller and his associates placed the stock of Standard of Ohio and its affiliates in other states under the control of a board of nine trustees, with Rockefeller at the head. They thus established the first major U.S. "trust" and set a pattern of organization for other monopolies.

The aggressive competitive practices of Standard Oil, which many regarded as ruthless, and the growing public hostility toward monopolies caused some industrialized states to enact antimonopoly laws and led to the passage by the U.S. Congress of the Sherman Antitrust Act in 1890. In 1892 the Ohio Supreme Court held that the Standard Oil Trust was a monopoly in violation of an Ohio law prohibiting monopolies. Rockefeller evaded the decision by dissolving the trust and transferring its properties to companies in other states, with interlocking directorates

John D. Rockefeller, 1930. Encyclopædia Britannica, Inc.

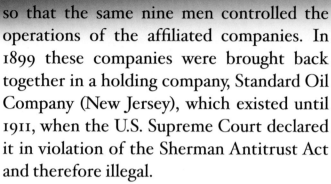

so that the same nine men controlled the operations of the affiliated companies. In 1899 these companies were brought back together in a holding company, Standard Oil Company (New Jersey), which existed until 1911, when the U.S. Supreme Court declared it in violation of the Sherman Antitrust Act and therefore illegal.

A devout Baptist, Rockefeller turned his attention increasingly during the 1890s to charities. After 1897 he devoted himself completely to philanthropy. He made possible the founding of the University of Chicago in 1892, and by the time of his death he had given it more than $80 million. In association with his son, John D. Rockefeller, Jr., he created major philanthropic institutions, including the Rockefeller Institute for Medical Research (renamed Rockefeller University) in New York City (1901); the General Education Board (1902); and the Rockefeller Foundation (1913). Rockefeller died in Ormond Beach, Fla., on May 23, 1937.

T he history of the industrialist and philanthropist Andrew Carnegie is one of the great American success stories. At 12 he was an immigrant boy earning $1.20 a week. Fifty years later he was giving away a third of a billion dollars of his own money. Meanwhile he had built up one of the world's largest steel companies.

Andrew Carnegie was born on Nov. 25, 1835, at Dunfermline near Edinburgh, Scotland. In 1848 the family came to America, settling at Allegheny, Pa. (now part of Pittsburgh). Young Andrew worked

Andrew Carnegie. **Library of Congress Prints and Photographs**

first as a bobbin boy in a cotton mill. Later he became a messenger in a telegraph office and then secretary to the superintendent of the Pennsylvania Railroad's Pittsburgh division. By the outbreak of the Civil War he himself was superintendent. He had also become a financier. Saving his earnings, he bought an interest in a sleeping-car company. The stock increased greatly in value when U.S. railroads adopted sleeping cars, and Carnegie made a great deal of money.

During the war he gave up his position to take charge of the eastern military railroads and telegraph lines for the government. After the Civil War he could see that iron bridges would soon replace wooden structures. So he founded the Keystone Bridge Works, which built the first iron bridge across the Ohio River. This business led him to found the iron and steel works that brought him the bulk of his huge fortune.

By 1899 Carnegie had consolidated many of the steel works located around Pittsburgh into the Carnegie Steel Company. Two years later, at the height of his phenomenal business career, he transferred his 500-million-dollar steel interests to the new United States Steel

Corporation. He then retired from business so that he could devote his time and money to public service.

Carnegie believed that it was the solemn duty of a rich man to redistribute his wealth in the public interest. He also felt, however, that indiscriminate giving was bad. "No person," he said, "and no community can be permanently helped except by their own cooperation."

To ensure that his money would be distributed wisely, he established the Carnegie Corporation of New York, with an endowment of $125 million. The income from this fund now goes to many causes. His biggest gift for any single purpose was the fund for establishing the Carnegie public libraries. Almost as famous are the Hero Funds he set up in many countries to recognize heroic acts that might otherwise go unappreciated.

Most of his fortune went to educational and scientific institutions. Many of these he founded himself. Among the other organizations were the Carnegie Endowment for International Peace, founded in 1910, and the Carnegie Foundation for the Advancement of Teaching, established in 1905.

Carnegie was devoted to his mother and supported her in luxurious fashion. He did not marry until after her death, when he was in his 50s. He and his wife bought a huge estate in Scotland and built a great house they called Skibo Castle. In his later years he was half-humorously known as the Laird of Skibo. Carnegie died at Shadowbrook, his summer home in Lenox, Mass., at the age of 83.

The first Carnegie Hero Fund Commission was established in Pittsburgh in 1904 with a grant of $5 million. Inscribed on the medal that its trustees award to persons who save — or attempt to save — the lives of others is the Biblical quotation, "Greater love hath no man than this, that a man lay down his life for his friends." Also in the philanthropist's memory, the Carnegie Medal has been awarded annually since 1937 for the best children's book published in the United Kingdom.

The first great labor leader in the United States was Samuel Gompers. He helped found the American Federation of Labor (AFL), which he developed from a group of 25 craft unions into a body of almost 150 unions.

Gompers was born in London on Jan. 27, 1850. He emigrated in 1863 from England to New York City, where he took up his father's trade of cigar making and in 1872 became a naturalized citizen. His careful leadership of labor interests earned Gompers a reputation for conservatism. In a period when the United States was bitterly hostile to labor organizations, he developed the principles of "voluntarism," which called for unions to exert coercion by economic actions—that is, through strikes and boycotts. In 1886 Gompers fostered the separation of the cigar makers and other craft unions from the Knights of Labor to form the AFL. He served as president of the AFL from 1886 to 1924 (except for one year, 1895). He distrusted intellectual reformers, fearing their influence

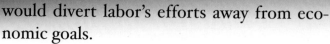

would divert labor's efforts away from economic goals.

Gompers is noted for having shifted the primary goal of American unionism away from social issues and toward the "bread and butter" issues of wages, benefits, hours, and working conditions, all of which could be negotiated through collective bargaining. Gompers' AFL became the model of unionism in the United States, achieving economic goals through national trade unions that organized a network of locals and supported them. He died in San Antonio, Tex., on Dec. 13, 1924.

An early concern for the living conditions of 19th-century factory workers led Jane Addams to assume a pioneering role in the field of social work. She brought cultural and day-care programs to the poor, sought justice for immigrants and blacks, championed labor reform, supported women's suffrage, and helped to train other social workers.

Jane Addams was born on Sept. 6, 1860, in Cedarville, Ill. Her father, John Huy Addams, was a wealthy miller, a state senator, and a friend of Abraham Lincoln. Jane was the youngest of five children. From infancy she suffered from a slight spinal curvature. After graduation from Rockford Seminary (now Rockford College) in Illinois, her health failed, and for two years she was an invalid.

In 1883 she went abroad to travel and to study. The hunger and misery she found in the great European cities impressed her more than their famous museums or historic relics. A childhood resolve to live among the poor was confirmed by a stay at Toynbee Hall in London, the world's first social settlement.

Jane Addams. **Hulton Archive/Getty Images**

In the fall of 1889 she settled with a school friend, Ellen Gates Starr, in a shabby old mansion on the Near West Side of Chicago among tenements and sweatshops. Their neighbors—people of a dozen races—called the place the "old Hull house" after its builder, Charles Hull. So Hull House was adopted as the name for what was to become the most famous social settlement in the United States.

At first the neighbors were suspicious and unfriendly, but they soon saw that Addams' friendliness was sincere and practical. A kindergarten and a day nursery were started. Wealthy people, university professors, students, and business executives contributed time and money to Hull House.

Hull House fed the hungry, nursed the sick, and guided the bewildered immigrant and the wayward child. Addams became a garbage inspector so that she could get the filthy streets cleaned up. She campaigned against the sweatshops and corrupt politicians. She and her associates at Hull House helped to pass the first factory legislation in Illinois and to establish in Chicago the world's first juvenile court.

Addams became one of the most deeply loved and famous Americans of her time. Universities presented her with honorary degrees. Visitors from all over the world came to see her at Hull House. Crowds in many countries heard her talk about her work.

During World War I Addams faced bitter criticism when she urged that the issues be settled by negotiation rather than by bloodshed. After the war she continued to spread her ideals as president of the Women's International League for Peace and Freedom. In 1931 she was awarded the Nobel Peace Prize jointly with Dr. Nicholas Murray Butler.

For 46 years Addams managed the settlement. Starr had been forced by ill health to retire about six years before the death of Addams on May 21, 1935. At the time of her death Hull House had been expanded to cover an entire city block, with buildings centered around a courtyard. In 1961 plans were laid to tear down Hull House to make room for a Chicago campus of the University of Illinois.

Despite vehement, worldwide protests against such plans, the properties were sold in 1963. The original building, however, was preserved as a memorial to Jane Addams.

Hull House settlement work has continued in new locations in Chicago.

Addams's best known writings are *Democracy and Social Ethics* (1902); *Newer Ideals of Peace* (1907); *The Spirit of Youth and the City Streets* (1909); *Twenty Years at Hull-House* (1910); *A New Conscience and an Ancient Evil* (1911); and *The Second Twenty Years at Hull-House* (1930).

A social reformer, journalist, photographer, and author, Jacob Riis shocked the United States with his photographs of slum conditions in the late 19th century. His efforts earned him the nickname Emancipator of the Slums.

Born in Ribe, Denmark, on May 3, 1849, Riis emigrated to the United States at the age of 21. There he held various jobs, gaining a firsthand acquaintance with the ragged underside of city life. In 1873 he became a police reporter assigned to New York City's Lower East Side, where he found that in some tenements the infant death rate was one in 10. Riis used the newly invented flashbulb technique in photographing the rooms and hallways of these buildings in order to dramatize his lectures and books.

Riis's photographs were published in 1890 in *How the Other Half Lives*, which made him famous. The response of the future U.S. president Theodore Roosevelt was: "I have read your book, and I have come to help." The book stimulated the first

significant New York laws to curb tenement house evils. The illustrations were largely line drawings based on Riis's photographs. A reprint in 1971 included 30 photographs on which the original illustrations were based and 70 related Riis photographs. Of Riis's many other books, the most noteworthy was his autobiography, *The Making of an American* (1901). Riis died in Barre, Mass., on May 26, 1914.

B ecause of the naturalist, explorer, and writer John Muir, the U.S. national park system was greatly expanded. In 1903 he took a camping trip in Yosemite with President Theodore Roosevelt, who absorbed Muir's

Yosemite National Park, California. © **Digital Vision/Getty Images**

enthusiasm for nature. During the remainder of Roosevelt's presidency, 148 million acres (60 million hectares) were set aside as national forests; 16 national monuments, including Muir Woods in California, were established; and the number of national parks doubled.

Muir was born on April 21, 1838, in Dunbar, Scotland. In 1849 the family emigrated to the United States and settled on a farm near Portage, Wis. In 1860 Muir entered the University of Wisconsin in Madison, but he left in 1863 without a degree because he studied only the subjects that interested him—chemistry, geology, and botany.

After leaving Madison, Muir worked on mechanical inventions. In 1867, however, an industrial accident nearly cost him an eye, causing him to abandon that career and devote himself to nature. He walked all the way from the Midwest to the Gulf of Mexico, keeping a journal as he went; after his death the journal was published as *A Thousand-Mile Walk to the Gulf*. In 1868 he went to the Yosemite Valley in California. From there he took many trips into Nevada, Utah, Oregon, Washington, and Alaska, inspired by his interest in glaciers and forests.

As early as 1876, Muir urged the federal government to adopt a forest conservation policy. He became a central figure in the debate over land use, advocating on behalf of

U.S. President Theodore Roosevelt and naturalist John Muir at Glacier Point, Yosemite Valley, Calif., **Encyclopædia Britannica, Inc.**

land preservation primarily through articles published in popular periodicals. Muir was largely responsible for the establishment of California's Sequoia and Yosemite national parks in 1890.

On May 28, 1892, Muir founded the Sierra Club, an organization devoted to protecting the environment. He served as its first president, a position he held until his death. He died in Los Angeles on Dec. 24, 1914.

CHAPTER 11

MARK TWAIN

A onetime printer and Mississippi River boat pilot, Mark Twain became one of America's greatest authors. His *Tom Sawyer*, *Huckleberry Finn*, and *Life on the Mississippi* rank high on any list of great American books.

The sixth child of John Marshall and Jane Lampton Clemens, Mark Twain was born Samuel Langhorne Clemens on Nov. 30, 1835, in the small town of Florida, Mo. His father was a hard worker but a poor provider. The family moved to Hannibal, Mo., on the Mississippi, when Samuel was 4 years old. It was in this river town that he grew up, and from it he gathered the material for his most famous stories.

His father died when he was 12, and the boy was apprenticed to a printer. In 1857 he apprenticed himself to a riverboat pilot. He became a licensed pilot and spent two and a half years at his new trade. The river swarmed with traffic, and the pilot was the most important person aboard the boat. He wrote of these years in *Life on the Mississippi*.

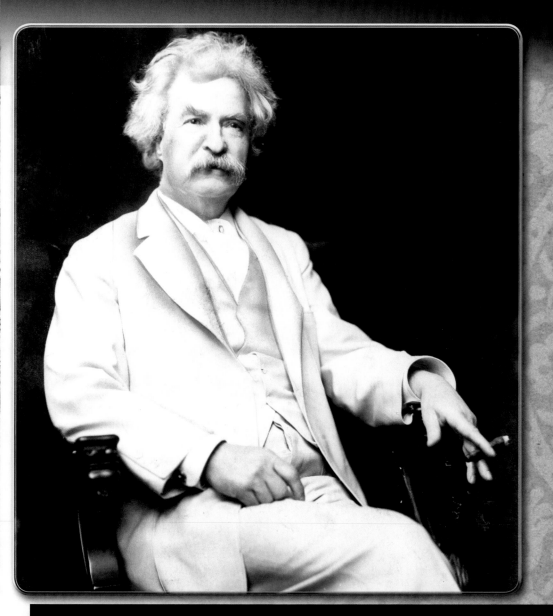

In his last decade, Mark Twain was an American folk hero and was in great demand as a public speaker. Library of Congress, Washington, D.C. LC-USZ62-112065

The Civil War ended his career as a pilot. Clemens went west to Nevada and soon became a reporter on the Virginia City newspaper. Here he began using the pen name Mark Twain. It is an old river term meaning two fathoms, or 12 feet (4 meters), of water depth.

In 1864 he went to California. The next year he wrote his "Jumping Frog" story, which ran in many newspapers. He was sent to the Sandwich Islands (now Hawaii) as a roving reporter, and on his return he began lecturing. He was soon on a tour of the Mediterranean and the Holy Land. From this came *The Innocents Abroad*, which made him famous.

In 1870 he married Olivia Langdon. She modified Twain's exaggerations, sometimes weakening his writings, sometimes actually making them more readable. Twain began turning out a new book every few years. William Dean Howells, editor of the *Atlantic Monthly* and a highly respected novelist, became his close friend and literary adviser.

Twain bought a publishing firm in Hartford, Conn. He earned much money writing, lecturing, and in his publishing house, but he spent it on high living and unsuccessful investments. He lost a fortune promoting a typesetting machine. By 1894 his publishing company had failed and he was bankrupt.

Twain set out on a world lecture tour to retrieve his fortune, and by 1898 his debts were paid. In his last years he traveled and spoke much but wrote comparatively little. He died on April 21, 1910.

Twain was more than a humorist. Behind his mask of humor lay a serious view of life. Tragedy had entered his own life in the poverty and early death of his father, the loss of a daughter, and his bankruptcy. His short story, "The Man That Corrupted Hadleyburg," published in 1900, which showed greed at work in a small town, is an indication of Twain's dark side.

The controversial *Huckleberry Finn*, which is periodically banned in schools or libraries because of alleged racial overtones, can be read by children, but it is not a child's book. It has elements of heartbreak and wisdom that can be appreciated best by adults. On the other hand, *Tom Sawyer* is primarily a juvenile book but one that can be read with pleasure by adults.

Twain's chief works are: *The Celebrated Jumping Frog of Calaveras County*, a collection published in 1867; *The Innocents Abroad* (1869); *Roughing It* (1872); *The Gilded Age*—with Charles Dudley Warner (1873); *The Adventures of Tom Sawyer* (1876); *A Tramp Abroad* (1880); *The Prince and the Pauper* (1882); *Life on the Mississippi* (1883); *The Adventures of Huckleberry Finn* (1884); *A Connecticut Yankee in King Arthur's Court* (1889); *The Tragedy of Pudd'nhead Wilson* (1894); and *Personal Recollections of Joan of Arc* (1896). Printed posthumously were: *The Mysterious Stranger* (1916); *Mark Twain's Notebook* (1935); and *Autobiography* (1959).

CHAPTER 12

HENRY JAMES

One of the most productive and influential American writers, Henry James was a master of fiction. He enlarged the form, was innovative with it, and placed upon it the mark of a highly individual method and style.

James was born on April 15, 1843, in New York City, the younger brother of noted philosopher and psychologist William James. He had two other brothers and one sister. His father, Henry, had inherited wealth, and the family enjoyed a life of leisure. The elder James lectured and wrote, largely about religious matters.

The James children were educated by private teachers, and Henry entered Harvard Law School in 1862. At first Henry seemed to have no definite idea of how he would use his many talents. He was just as interested in drawing and mathematics as he was in writing. At Harvard, however, under the influence of Charles Eliot Norton and William Dean Howells, he decided that literature would be his life's work.

Henry James. **Hulton Archive/Getty Images**

From 1865 to 1869 he wrote criticism and short stories. After much travel, he decided in 1875 to live in Europe. He went first to Paris but in 1876 settled in London. James received an honorary degree from Harvard in 1911 and one from Oxford in 1912. Angry at the United States for not entering World War I at its start, he became a British citizen in 1915.

Because he wrote of a society of sophistication and culture, Henry James was accused of being a snobbish writer. He maintained, however, that it was only this kind of society that had the leisure to indulge in the delicate personal relationships in which he was interested. He wrote of these relationships with great psychological skill and in precise language, usually seeking to involve the reader in the thoughts and outlook of one character.

James wrote 20 novels, 112 shorter works, and 12 plays. The theme of much of his writing was the clash between the innocence and exuberance of the New World with the corruption and wisdom of the Old. His themes also included personal relationships, which he explored in *The Portrait of a*

Lady, published in 1881, and social reform, of which he wrote in *The Bostonians* and *The Princess Casamassima* (both 1886). Some of his other works included *Daisy Miller* (1878), *Washington Square* (1880), *The Turn of the Screw* (1898), *The Wings of the Dove* (1902), and *The Ambassadors* (1903). James died on Feb. 28, 1916, in London. His ashes were taken to the United States and buried in Cambridge, Mass.

CHAPTER 13

Writer and critic William Dean Howells was for many years regarded as the dean of American literature. He was a magazine editor who wrote numerous novels in addition to farces and comedies, essays, criticism, and poems. He used his considerable influence to promote the school of realism in American fiction.

Howells was born in Martins Ferry, Ohio, on March 1, 1837. His father traveled around Ohio working as a printer and journalist. When young Howells was 9 he began to set type in his father's shop. He did not attend high school or college, but he studied foreign languages and literature at home. Between 1856 and 1861 he worked on the *Ohio State Journal* in Columbus as a reporter and editor. In 1860 he published a book of poems. It was a campaign biography of Abraham Lincoln, however, that really launched Howells's career. He used the money he made from that project to go to New England, where he met such writers as James Russell Lowell and Ralph Waldo Emerson. In 1861 Lincoln, having become president, named Howells consul at Venice. In 1862 Howells married his Columbus sweetheart, Elinor G. Mead, in Paris. They had two daughters and a son.

After returning to the United States in 1865, he worked in Boston as assistant editor of the *Atlantic Monthly*. In 1871 he became editor in chief. That same year he published his first novel, *Their Wedding Journey*. Howells left the *Atlantic* in 1881 to devote himself to writing. In 1891 he moved to New York City and for a few months was editor of *Cosmopolitan Magazine*. Later he went to *Harper's Monthly*, where from 1900 until his death he conducted "The Editor's Easy Chair," a review of contemporary life and letters. He was the first president of the American Academy of Arts and Letters. His best-known novels include *A Foregone Conclusion*, published in 1875; *The Lady of Aroostook* (1879); *The Rise of Silas Lapham* (1885); *Indian Summer* (1886); and *A Hazard of New Fortunes* (1889). He died on May 11, 1920, in New York City.

The upper-class society into which Edith Wharton was born provided her with abundant material for plotting her novels and short stories. Her major literary model was Henry James, a close friend in her later years. Like him, she lived a great part of her life in Europe, rarely returning to the United States after 1907.

Wharton was born Edith Newbold Jones in New York City on Jan. 24, 1862. She was educated by private tutors at home and in Europe. She married Boston banker Edward Wharton in 1885. Her first novel, *The Valley of Decision*, was published in 1902. Critical acclaim came with *The House of Mirth* in 1905. It analyzed the aristocratic society she knew and its reaction to social change.

A similar theme was evident in *The Custom of the Country* (1913), *Twilight Sleep* (1927), *Hudson River Bracketed* (1929), and *The Gods Arrive* (1932). Her most enduring novel was *Ethan Frome* (1911), which explored the grim and often anguished nature of New England farm life. *The Age of Innocence*

Edith Wharton. **Fotosearch/Archive Photos/Getty Images**

(1920), which won a Pulitzer prize, is considered her finest work.

She divorced Wharton in 1913. In 1923, on her last visit to the United States, she became the first woman to receive an honorary doctorate from Yale University. In all, she published more than 50 books, including fiction, poetry, travel books, and literary criticism. She died on Aug. 11, 1937, in St-Brice-sous-Forêt, France.

CHAPTER 15

THOMAS EAKINS

As has been true for so many great art-
ists, the work of Thomas Eakins was
not appreciated in his lifetime. No museum
bought one of his paintings until 1916, the
year he died. Nor was there a major exhibi-
tion of his work until a year later. Today he
is considered one of the masters of American
realism.

Thomas Eakins was born on July 25,
1844, in Philadelphia, the city where he
would spend most of his life. He studied
at the Pennsylvania Academy of Fine Arts,
and, because of his special interest in painting the human figure, he attended lectures
in anatomy at Jefferson Medical College.
From 1866 to 1869 he studied in Paris at the
École des Beaux-Arts (School of Fine Arts),
where he gained a solid background in traditional art. He ignored all of the experimental,
avant-garde work of the French impression-
ists and pursued his own interest in realism.
After a brief visit to Spain, he returned to
Philadelphia in 1870.

Self-portrait of Thomas Eakins. National Academy Museum, New York, USA/The Bridgeman Art Library

Eakins was a man of varied interests: painting, sculpture, anatomy, music, photography, and the study of locomotion. In the 1880s he experimented with multiple-image photography of moving animals and athletes. His interest in motion also led him to paint an impressive series of boxing scenes.

Nearly all of his work was portraiture—depictions of people he knew. His paintings demonstrated his technical expertise with external and anatomical details, combined with representations of inner character and situation. His first subjects were members of his family and an assortment of friends. Among his outdoor scenes were *Max Schmitt in a Single Scull* and *The Swimming Hole*.

Eakins was invited to provide a painting for the Philadelphia Centennial Exposition of 1876. He painted a work entitled *The Gross Clinic*, showing the physician Samuel Gross performing surgery before a class of medical students. Now generally considered Eakins's masterpiece, it was rejected for the exposition.

From the late 1870s until 1886 he taught at the Pennsylvania Academy of Fine Arts.

Eventually he was forced to resign, mostly over the notoriety caused by his insistence on using live, nude models in classes of both men and women. He continued to teach from time to time at the new Art Students League and at the National Academy of Design in New York City. He died on June 25, 1916.

Democrats from all parts of the country crowded into Washington to witness the presidential inauguration of March 4, 1885. For the first time since the Civil War a Democrat had won the presidency. Grover Cleveland, an honest and principled politician, had revived the party. Elected again in 1892, he was both the 22nd and the 24th president of the United States. He was the only president ever to be reelected after a defeat.

EARLY LIFE

Stephen Grover Cleveland was born in Caldwell, N.J., on March 18, 1837. He grew up in New Jersey and later in New York State. When his father died in 1853, Grover had to give up school to support his mother and sisters. He spent a year teaching young children at the New York Institution for the Blind. Then he decided to look for a job with more opportunity for advancement.

In Buffalo, N.Y., Grover worked as a clerk in a law office. He received no salary

Grover Cleveland. Stock Montage/Archive Photos/Getty Images

but was allowed to study in the firm's library. He passed the examination to be a lawyer in 1859, when he was 22 years old.

POLITICAL CAREER

Before he was old enough to vote, Cleveland had become an active worker in the Democratic party. In 1863 he was appointed assistant district attorney for Erie County, and from 1870 to 1873 he served as county sheriff. In 1881 he was elected mayor of Buffalo. He became known as the "veto mayor" because he vetoed so many dishonest bills.

Cleveland had served only one year as mayor when a Democratic reform group began to look around for a principled candidate for governor to oppose New York City's Tammany Hall politicians. Cleveland received the nomination and crushed his Republican opponent. As governor he broke openly with Tammany, earning himself a national reputation.

In 1884 the Democrats nominated Cleveland for the presidency. With his reputation for honesty, Cleveland contrasted sharply with his Republican opponent, James G. Blaine, who was known for political

contest.

FIRST TERM AND DEFEAT

As president, Cleveland took a firm stand against corruption and extravagance. He upheld the Civil Service Commission against members of his own party who were eager for the spoils of office. He read carefully each private pension bill for Civil War veterans and vetoed hundreds. After the Interstate Commerce Act of 1887 was passed, he gave close attention to forming the Interstate Commerce Commission, the first regulatory agency in the United States.

Shortly after his election, Cleveland began a concentrated study of the tariff. In 1887 he devoted his entire annual message to Congress to attacking the high tariff and the trusts it protected. Cleveland was renominated in 1888 and made tariff reform the chief issue of the campaign. He won about 100,000 more votes than the Republican candidate, Benjamin Harrison, but Harrison won 233 electoral votes to Cleveland's 168.

Cleveland spent the next four years working for a prominent law firm in New York City.

He watched the Harrison Administration spending money recklessly and making what he regarded as dangerous blunders. The McKinley Tariff of 1890 raised rates so high that imports almost stopped. The Sherman Silver Purchase Act of 1890 caused a steady outflow of gold from the treasury. As Harrison's term drew to a close, the country was sliding swiftly into a serious agricultural and industrial depression.

In 1892 the Democrats again nominated Cleveland for the presidency. This time he easily defeated Harrison.

SECOND TERM

Two months after the inauguration, the great Panic of 1893 swept the country. Banks closed their doors, railroads went bankrupt, and farm mortgages were foreclosed. People hoarded gold, and the treasury was fast losing its gold reserve.

Cleveland called a special session of Congress to deal with the currency situation. The president stood for the gold standard and succeeded in having the Sherman Silver Purchase Act repealed.

Yet the depression only worsened, and Cleveland's popularity sank. There were strikes in mines, on railroads, and in textile mills. In 1894 a strike in Chicago against the Pullman railroad car company turned violent. Cleveland sent in federal troops to end the strike, a decision that lost him the support of many workers.

Cleveland was unyielding in his opposition to foreign expansion. In 1893 he withdrew from the Senate a treaty calling for the annexation of Hawaii. In 1895, when the Cubans revolted against Spain, he held firmly to neutrality.

RETIREMENT

When his second term drew to a close, Cleveland retired to Princeton, N.J. He became active in the affairs of Princeton University as a lecturer in public affairs and as a trustee. Gradually public opinion changed, and Cleveland regained much of the public admiration he had earlier enjoyed. In 1904 he saw the Democratic party declare for the gold standard. He died at Westland on June 24, 1908.

CHAPTER 17

IDA B. WELLS–BARNETT

Journalist and civil rights advocate Ida B. Wells-Barnett led an antilynching crusade in the United States in the 1890s. She used both the newspaper and lectures to get her message across. Wells-Barnett was militant in her demand for justice for African Americans and in her insistence that it was to be won by their own efforts.

Ida Bell Wells was born on July 16, 1862, in Holly Springs, Miss., the daughter of slaves. She was educated at Rust University, a freedmen's school in Holly Springs, and at age 14 began teaching in a country school. After moving to Memphis, Tenn., in 1884, Wells continued to teach. She also attended Fisk University in Nashville during several summer sessions. In 1887 Tennessee's supreme court ruled against her in a suit she had brought against a railroad that tried to force her to leave a "whites-only" car. A few years later Wells, using the pen name Iola, wrote some newspaper articles that criticized the education that was available to African

Ida B. Wells-Barnett. R. Gates/Getty Images

American children. Her teaching contract was not renewed. She then turned to journalism, buying an interest in the *Memphis Free Speech*.

In 1892, after three friends of hers had been lynched by a mob, Wells began an editorial campaign against lynching. Although her newspaper's office was sacked, she continued her antilynching crusade, first as a writer for the *New York Age* and then as a lecturer and organizer of antilynching societies. She traveled to many major U.S. cities and twice visited Great Britain to spread her message. In 1895 she married Ferdinand L. Barnett, a Chicago lawyer, editor, and public official, and adopted the name Wells-Barnett. After that she concentrated her efforts in Chicago. She contributed to the *Chicago Conservator*, her husband's newspaper, and published a detailed look at lynching in *A Red Record* (1895). Wells-Barnett also helped organize local African American women in various causes, from the antilynching campaign to the suffrage movement. She founded Chicago's Alpha Suffrage Club, which may have been the first black woman suffrage group.

From 1898 to 1902 Wells-Barnett served as secretary of the National Afro-American Council. In 1910 she founded and became the first president of the Negro Fellowship League, which helped newly arrived migrants from the South. From 1913 to 1916 she worked as a probation officer of the Chicago municipal court. Wells-Barnett died in Chicago on March 25, 1931.

For more than half a century Susan B. Anthony fought for women's right to vote. Many people made fun of her. Some insulted her. Nevertheless, she traveled from county to county in New York and other states making speeches and organizing clubs for women's rights. She pleaded her cause with every president from Abraham Lincoln to Theodore Roosevelt.

Susan Brownell Anthony was born on Feb. 15, 1820, in Adams, Mass. When she was 6 years old her family moved to Battenville, N.Y. She attended a school set up by her father and later a boarding school near Philadelphia. After teaching at a female academy in upstate New York (1846–49), she settled in her family home, now near Rochester, N.Y. In the 1850s she became active in the temperance movement and an ardent abolitionist. When blacks were given the right to vote by the 15th Amendment, she launched a campaign to extend the same right to women. In 1869 she helped to organize the National Woman Suffrage Association.

Susan B. Anthony. **Hulton Archive/Getty Images**

To test her status as a citizen, Anthony voted in the presidential election of 1872. For this act she was tried and fined $100, but she refused to pay the fine, declaring that "taxation without representation is tyranny." In 1890 the National Woman Suffrage Association joined the American Woman Suffrage Association to form the National American Woman Suffrage Association. She became the president of the new association in 1892 and held this office until she was 80 years old.

Anthony died in Rochester, N.Y., on March 13, 1906. After her death both major political parties endorsed women's suffrage. In 1920 the Nineteenth Amendment to the U.S. Constitution was ratified, giving women the right to vote.

CHAPTER 19

In 1896 a horseless carriage chugged along the streets of Detroit, with crowds gathering whenever it appeared. Terrified horses ran at its approach. The police tried to curb this nuisance by forcing its driver, Henry Ford, to get a license. That car was the first of many millions produced by the automotive pioneer.

Henry Ford was born near Dearborn, Mich., on July 30, 1863. His mother died when he was 12. He helped on the family farm in summer and in winter attended a one-room school. Watches and clocks fascinated the boy. He went around the countryside doing repair work without pay, merely for the chance to tinker with machinery.

At 16 Ford walked to Detroit and apprenticed himself to a mechanic for $2.50 a week. His board was $3.50, so he worked four hours every night for a watchmaker for $2 a week. Later he worked in an engine shop and set up steam engines used on farms. In 1884 he took charge of a farm his father gave him.

He married and seemed settled down, but after two years he went back to Detroit and worked as night engineer for the Detroit Edison Company.

Ford built his first car in a little shed behind his home. It had a two-cylinder engine over the rear axle that developed four horsepower, a single seat fitted in a boxlike body, an electric bell for a horn, and a steering lever instead of a wheel. In 1899 Ford helped organize the Detroit Automobile Company, which built cars to order. Ford wanted to build in quantity at a price within the reach of many. His partners objected, and Ford withdrew.

In 1903 he organized the Ford Motor Company with only $28,000 raised in cash. This money came from 11 other stockholders. One investor put just $2,500 into Ford's venture (only $1,000 of it in cash). He drew more than $5 million in dividends, and he received more than $30 million when he sold all of his holdings to Ford in 1919.

Early automobile manufacturers merely bought automobile parts and assembled the cars. Ford's objective was to make every part that went into his cars. He acquired iron and coal mines, forests, mills, and factories to produce and shape his steel and alloys, his fuel,

The winning Model T Ford entry pauses on a rutted road during the transcontinental race from New York City to Seattle in 1909. **Courtesy of Ford Motor Company Archives**

wood, glass, and leather. He built railroad and steamship lines and an airplane freight service in order to transport his products.

Mass production was Ford's main idea, and he replaced men with machines wherever possible. Each man was given only one task, which he did repeatedly until it became automatic. Conveyors brought the job to the man instead of having the man waste time going to the job. To cut shipping costs, parts were shipped from the main plants in the Detroit area and assembled into cars at branch plants.

Ford also won fame as a philanthropist and pacifist. He established an eight-hour day, a minimum wage of $5 daily (later raised to $6), and a five-day week. He built a hospital in Detroit with fixed rates for service and physicians and nurses on salary. He created the Edison Institute, which includes Greenfield Village and the Edison Institute Museum and trade schools. Independence Hall, Thomas Edison's early laboratory, and other famous old buildings were reproduced in the village, which is open to the public. During World War I Ford headed a party of pacifists to Norway in a failed attempt to end the war, but during both World War I and World War II his company was a major producer of war materials.

In 1945 Ford yielded the presidency of the company to his 28-year-old grandson, Henry Ford II. Ford died on April 7, 1947, at the age of 83. Most of his personal estate, valued at about $205 million, was left to the Ford Foundation, one of the world's largest public trusts.

The 25th president of the United States was William McKinley. He was the leader of the country when, at the end of the 19th century, it suddenly became a world power by making territorial acquisitions overseas following the Spanish-American War.

EARLY LIFE

William McKinley, the son of William and Nancy Allison McKinley, was born in Niles, Ohio, on Jan. 29, 1843. When he was nine, the family moved to Poland, Ohio. At age 17 William entered Allegheny College at Meadville, Pa. He remained only a few months, returning home because of ill health. Then feeling that he could not afford to continue in college, he taught in a country school near Poland. After school hours he worked as a clerk in the Poland post office.

When the Civil War broke out in 1861, McKinley enlisted in an Ohio regiment led by Rutherford B. Hayes, later to become president of the United States. After the war

William McKinley. **Stock Montage/Archive Photos/Getty Images**

McKinley studied law for two years and then began a practice in Canton, Ohio.

POLITICAL CAREER

Drawn to politics, McKinley won his first public office in 1869, when the young Republican was elected prosecuting attorney in a Democratic county. In 1876 he was elected to the U.S. House of Representatives. He remained there for 14 years, except for one interval after the election of 1882. He rose steadily in the organization of the Republican party.

Many of the people he represented in Ohio were manufacturers. McKinley believed that a high tariff would build up American industry and bring prosperity to people of all classes. As chairman of the Ways and Means Committee, he was the author of the tariff law of 1890 known as the McKinley Act. It was the first time the tariff was systematically revised to protect all American manufacturers.

From 1892 to 1896 McKinley was governor of Ohio. During this period he continued to take an active part in national party affairs, aiming at the Republican nomination for the

91

presidency in 1896. McKinley was supported in this ambition by Mark Hanna, a wealthy Ohio industrialist and political leader. He managed the campaign and was chiefly responsible for McKinley's nomination. William Jennings Bryan was the Democratic nominee.

The campaign was fought on an issue other than the tariff. The Republicans believed in a money system based on the single gold standard. The Democrats believed in bimetallism—that is, a money system based on both gold and silver. Bryan had the support of poor farmers and other people in debt, who would benefit from the unlimited coinage of silver. Behind McKinley were the bankers and manufacturers. McKinley won the election decisively.

PRESIDENCY

Immediately after his inauguration McKinley called a special meeting of Congress to consider tariff revision. Within three days a bill known as the Dingley Tariff Act once more raised the tariff on many imported items. Yet domestic issues would play only a minor role in McKinley's presidency. Americans were

role on the world stage. Under McKinley, the United States became an empire.

In February 1898 the U.S. battleship *Maine* exploded in the harbor of Havana, Cuba, with a loss of 260 lives. This was a climax to years of trouble between Cuba and its despotic ruler, Spain. The *Maine* had been sent to Havana to protect Americans in case war should break out between Cuba and Spain. McKinley made every effort to avoid war, and a mid-20th century investigation would later prove that the ship was destroyed by an internal explosion. Nevertheless, the "yellow" (sensational) newspapers inflamed popular opinion against Spain. Even the assistant secretary of the Navy, Theodore Roosevelt, strongly urged war. McKinley was forced to recommend to Congress that the United States free Cuba by force, and war was declared on April 25.

The brief Spanish-American War ended with the Paris Peace Treaty of Dec. 10, 1898, which gave Puerto Rico, Guam, and the Philippines to the United States and liberated Cuba. The new responsibilities brought the United States into closer contact with the great powers of Europe and Asia.

REELECTION AND DEATH

Through his first four years, President McKinley continued to grow in popularity. The successful war and the country's prosperity weakened any opposition to his administration. There was no doubt of McKinley's renomination in 1900. In the election he soundly defeated Bryan, the Democratic nominee, for a second time.

Following his inauguration in 1901, McKinley left Washington for a speaking tour of the western states. In September 1901, at the Pan-American Exposition in Buffalo, N.Y., he spoke of the possibility of lowering tariffs by reciprocal treaties among countries. On September 6, the day following his address, McKinley held a public reception at the exposition. An anarchist, Leon Czolgosz, fired two shots into the president's chest and abdomen. Rushed to a hospital in Buffalo, McKinley lingered for a week before dying in the early morning hours of September 14.

A lthough he was defeated three times for the presidency of the United States, William Jennings Bryan molded public opinion as few presidents have done. For many years he was the leader of the Democratic

William Jennings Bryan. **Hulton Archive/Archive Photos/ Getty Images**

party, and it was his influence that won the Democratic presidential nomination for Woodrow Wilson in 1912.

Bryan was born in Salem, Ill. He went to school and practiced law in Illinois until 1887, when he moved to Nebraska. There he built up a reputation as a great orator and was elected to Congress.

Six years later, in 1896 at the age of 36, Bryan achieved national fame—he received his first nomination for the presidency. He won in the national Democratic convention by a vigorous appeal for free and unlimited coinage of silver. Turning to those who wanted only gold as the money standard, he exclaimed: "You shall not press down upon the brow of labor this crown of thorns. You shall not crucify mankind upon this cross of gold."

Though Bryan lost the election then and again in 1900 and 1908, he was still regarded as the leader of the Democratic party. Through his paper, called *The Commoner*, and by lectures delivered from Chautauqua platforms he advanced the cause of prohibition, of religion, and of morality.

Bryan was named secretary of state by President Wilson. He negotiated treaties with 30 countries, representing three-fourths of the world's population, for investigation of disputes before resorting to war. Because of his opposition to war, he resigned from office in June 1915 in protest against the president's firmness concerning the sinking of the *Lusitania*.

After the war he moved to Florida and worked to advance moral and religious causes. He died in July 1925, in Dayton, Tenn., where he had been helping prosecute a case involving an "anti-evolution" law.

CHAPTER 22

WILLIAM RANDOLPH HEARST

Through dishonest and exaggerated reporting, William Randolph Hearst's newspapers whipped up public sentiment against Spain, actually helping to cause the Spanish-American War. Hearst was quite willing to take credit for this, as his New York City newspaper testified in an 1898 headline: "How Do You Like the *Journal*'s War?" His controversial life became the subject of the motion picture *Citizen Kane* (1941).

Hearst was born in San Francisco on April 29, 1863. His father, George Hearst, was a gold-mine owner as well as U.S. senator (1886–91). Hearst attended Harvard University for two years before taking control of the failing *San Francisco Examiner* in 1887. His father had bought the paper in 1880. He turned the newspaper into a paying venture before entering the New York City market to compete with publisher Joseph Pulitzer.

Hearst bought the *New York Morning Journal* in 1895. The paper soon attained

William Randolph Hearst. Hulton Archive/Archive Photos/ Getty Images

an unprecedented circulation through its one-cent price, use of illustrations, color magazine sections, comic strips, and its glaring and sensational headlines. The term *yellow journalism* was coined to define the type of sensationalism and, often, irresponsibility exhibited by Hearst and Pulitzer. In 1896 Hearst introduced the *New York Evening Journal*. In 1897–98 he relentlessly promoted the need to fight a war with Spain over Cuba.

His publishing empire grew as he acquired the *Chicago American*, the *Chicago Examiner*, and the *Boston American*. By 1925 he owned newspapers in every section of the United States. He also bought a number of magazines, including *Cosmopolitan*, the *World Today*, and *Harper's Bazaar*. He published books, chiefly fiction, and produced a number of motion pictures. The films were primarily vehicles for Marion Davies, his mistress for more than 30 years. He built himself a grandiose castle in San Simeon, Calif.

Hearst's political ambitions won him two terms in the U.S. House of Representatives (1903–07), and he was nearly elected mayor of New York City in 1905. During the Great Depression of the 1930s his publishing empire began to disintegrate, and many publications were sold. World War II restored his fortunes, however, and the newspapers and magazines prospered again. Hearst died in Beverly Hills, Calif., on Aug. 14, 1951. His son Randolph A. Hearst succeeded him in business.

CHAPTER 23

BOOKER T. WASHINGTON

The first African American whose face appeared on a U.S. postage stamp was Booker T. Washington, who was thus honored a quarter century after his death. His 10-cent stamp went on sale in 1940 at Tuskegee Institute, which Washington had founded when he was only 25 years old. The educator's monument on its campus shows him lifting a symbolic veil from the head of a freed slave.

Booker Taliaferro Washington was born a slave on April 5, 1856, in Franklin County, Va. His mother, Jane Burroughs, was a plantation cook. His father was an unknown white man. As a child, Booker swept yards and brought water to slaves working in the fields. Freed after the Civil War, he went with his mother to Malden, W. Va., to join Washington Ferguson, whom she had married during the war.

Booker helped support the family by working in salt and coal mines. He taught himself the alphabet, then studied nights with the teacher of a local school for blacks. When he began attending the school, he

Booker T. Washington. Library of Congress, Washington, D.C.

had to work five hours each day before class. He called himself Booker Washington until he learned that his mother had named him Booker Taliaferro.

At about age 16 Booker set out for Hampton Normal and Agricultural Institute, which had been established by the chief of the Freedmen's Bureau to educate former slaves. He walked much of the way, working to earn the fare to complete the long, dusty journey to Virginia. For his admission test he repeatedly swept and dusted a classroom, and he was able to earn his board by working as a janitor. After graduation three years later he taught in Malden and at Hampton.

In 1880 the Alabama state legislature approved the establishment of a school in Tuskegee for training African American teachers. When the board of commissioners asked the head of Hampton to send a principal, they expected the principal to be white. Instead Washington arrived in June 1881. He began classes in July with 30 students in a shanty donated by a black church. Later he borrowed money to buy an abandoned plantation nearby and moved the school there. By the time of his death in Tuskegee in 1915 the institute (now a university) had some buildings, and a large faculty.

Washington believed that blacks could promote their constitutional rights by impressing Southern whites with their economic and moral progress. He wanted them to forget about political power and concentrate on their farming skills and learning industrial trades. Brickmaking, mattress making, and wagon building were among the courses Tuskegee offered. Its all-black faculty included the famous agricultural scientist George Washington Carver.

Washington's conciliatory policy appealed to white politicians, many of whom contributed money to Tuskegee. He became an adviser to U.S. presidents on racial issues and on the appointment of blacks to government positions. Blacks in the South were motivated by his self-help programs, but militant blacks in the North, including W.E.B. Du Bois, criticized his attitude toward racial segregation and discrimination. They argued that higher education, rather than vocational training, and political agitation would eventually win full civil rights.

The open controversy over acceptable black leadership dated from 1895,

when Washington was invited to address a white audience at the Cotton States and International Exposition in Atlanta, Ga. While emphasizing the importance of economic advancement to blacks, he repeatedly used the paraphrase, "Cast down your bucket where you are." Some blacks were incensed by his comment, "The wisest among my race understand that the agitation of questions of social equality is the extremest folly."

Washington received honorary degrees from Harvard University and Dartmouth College. Among his publications were *Up from Slavery* (1901), his autobiography, and *Frederick Douglass* (1907). Married three times, he outlived his first two wives. He died on Nov. 14, 1915.

For more than 50 years W. E. B. Du Bois, an editor, historian, and sociologist, was a leader of the civil rights movement in the United States. He helped found the National Association for the Advancement of Colored People (NAACP) and was its outstanding spokesman in the first decades of its existence.

William Edward Burghardt Du Bois was born on Feb. 23, 1868, in Great Barrington, Mass. His parents, Alfred and Mary Burghardt Du Bois, were of African and European ancestry. An excellent student, Du Bois graduated from Fisk University in 1888 and from Harvard College in 1890. He traveled in Europe and studied at the University of Berlin. In 1895 he received a Ph.D. from Harvard. His dissertation, *The Suppression of the African Slave-Trade to the United States of America, 1638–1870*, was published in 1896 as the first volume of the Harvard Historical Studies.

After teaching Greek and Latin at Wilberforce University from 1894 to 1896,

W. E. B. Du Bois. **Hulton Archive/Archive Photos/Getty Images**

Philadelphia Negro, published in 1899, a pioneering sociological study, he hoped to dispel the ignorance of whites about blacks, which he believed was a cause of racial prejudice. Du Bois taught at Atlanta University from 1897 to 1910 and from 1897 until 1914 directed its annual studies of black life.

In *The Souls of Black Folk* (1903), Du Bois declared that "the problem of the Twentieth Century is the problem of the color-line." He criticized the famous black educator Booker T. Washington for accepting racial discrimination and minimizing the value of college training for blacks. Du Bois felt that blacks needed higher education for leadership. In his essay "The Talented Tenth" he wrote, "The Negro race, like all races, is going to be saved by its exceptional men."

The split between Washington and Du Bois reflected a bitter division of opinion among black leaders. In 1905, at Niagara Falls, Canada, Du Bois joined the more militant leaders to demand equal voting rights and educational opportunities for blacks and an end to racial discrimination. But the Niagara Movement declined within a few years, and he then helped form another group, which

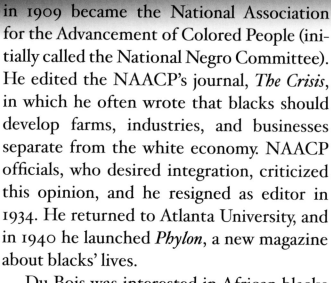

in 1909 became the National Association for the Advancement of Colored People (initially called the National Negro Committee). He edited the NAACP's journal, *The Crisis*, in which he often wrote that blacks should develop farms, industries, and businesses separate from the white economy. NAACP officials, who desired integration, criticized this opinion, and he resigned as editor in 1934. He returned to Atlanta University, and in 1940 he launched *Phylon*, a new magazine about blacks' lives.

Du Bois was interested in African blacks and led several Pan-African congresses. He was awarded the Spingarn medal in 1920 for his efforts to foster black racial solidarity. Although he clashed with Marcus Garvey, the leader of a "back to Africa" movement, and attacked his scheme for an African empire, he lauded Garvey's racial pride.

In his later years Du Bois came to believe that the United States could not solve its racial problems and that the only world power opposed to racial discrimination was the Soviet Union. He was awarded the Communist-sponsored International Peace prize in 1952 and the Soviet Lenin Peace prize in 1958. Du Bois joined the Communist party of the United States in 1961 and emigrated to Ghana, where he became a citizen, in 1963. He died there on Aug. 27, 1963. He had been married twice, to Nina Gomer and to Shirley Graham, and had two children.

Du Bois was brilliant, proud, and aloof. He once wrote: "My leadership was a leadership of ideas. I never was, nor ever will be, personally popular." Du Bois wrestled with his conflicting desires for both integration and black nationalism. His Pan-African and Communist views removed him from the mainstream of the U.S. civil rights movement. But he never wavered in his efforts to teach blacks their rights as human beings and pride in their heritage. Among his writings are *Black Reconstruction* (1935) and *Dusk of Dawn* (1940).

CHAPTER 25

THEODORE ROOSEVELT

The youngest president of the United States was Theodore Roosevelt. He had been vice president under William McKinley. He came into office in 1901, just before his 43rd birthday, when McKinley was killed by an anarchist. He was elected in his own right in 1904. As president, Roosevelt championed progressive reforms and made the United States a strong presence in international affairs. A man of tremendous energy and high spirits, he was not only a statesman but also a soldier, naturalist, and writer.

EARLY LIFE

Theodore Roosevelt was born on Oct. 27, 1858, in New York City. His family was wealthy and socially prominent. Sickly as a boy, Theodore was educated by private tutors. From an early age he displayed a wide-ranging intellectual curiosity, but he was especially interested in natural history.

Theodore Roosevelt. **Fotosearch/Archive Photos/Getty Images**

He graduated from Harvard College in 1880. In the same year he married Alice Lee, with whom he had a daughter.

Though physically weak during his youth, Roosevelt later developed a strong physique through exercise. He became a lifelong advocate of vigorous physical and mental activity, advising everyone to lead "the strenuous life."

POLITICAL CAREER

Roosevelt studied briefly at Columbia Law School but soon turned to writing and politics as a career. In 1881, when he was only 23 years old, he was elected as a Republican to the New York legislature. In spite of his youth he quickly earned respect for his opposition to corrupt, party-machine politics. In 1884, overcome by grief by the deaths of both his mother and his wife on the same day, he left politics to spend two years on his cattle ranch in the Badlands of the Dakota Territory. He threw himself into the rough life of the frontier, rounding up cattle, hunting, and sometimes serving as deputy sheriff.

playmate, Edith Carow, in London and settled down to a new life at Sagamore Hill, an estate near Oyster Bay on Long Island, New York. They had five children.

Roosevelt began writing a history, *The Winning of the West*. But when President Benjamin Harrison offered him the position of civil service commissioner in 1889, he moved to Washington and for six years worked for civil-service reform. In 1895 he took the post of police commissioner in New York City. In this position he tried to put an end to graft and corruption in the police force, though his efforts were opposed by politicians and newspapers alike.

After two years Roosevelt resigned to become assistant secretary of the Navy under President William McKinley. As war with Spain neared, Roosevelt, on his own authority, quietly ordered preparations. When war was declared he organized the 1st Volunteer Cavalry regiment. They were called Rough Riders because many of them were cowboys. Roosevelt was acclaimed a national hero when he led the daring charge

on San Juan Hill) in Cuba.

Roosevelt came home to be elected governor of New York in 1898. He became an energetic reformer, removing corrupt officials and enacting legislation to regulate corporations and the civil service. Fearing him as a candidate for the presidency, the Republican bosses succeeded in putting him in the post with the most unpromising future—that of vice president of the United States when McKinley was reelected in 1900. In 1901, however, McKinley was assassinated, elevating Roosevelt to the presidency. In 1904 he easily won a full term.

PRESIDENCY

From what he called the presidency's "bully pulpit," Roosevelt gave speeches about the country's role in world politics, the need for economic reforms, and the impact of political corruption. At home he worked for peaceful relations between businesses and workers—a program he called the Square Deal. In foreign affairs Roosevelt's policy was to "speak softly and carry a big stick." By this he meant that the United States should deal fairly with other countries but also be ready to protect its interests.

One of Roosevelt's early domestic initiatives was to urge enforcement of the Sherman Antitrust Act of 1890 against industrial monopolies, popularly known as "trusts." Railroad mergers had produced huge monopolies. In 1903 Roosevelt brought suit under the Sherman Antitrust Act for the dissolution of a railroad conglomerate, the Northern Securities Company. The United States won the suit. Roosevelt continued this policy of "trust-busting" by beginning suits against the United States Steel Corporation, the Standard Oil Company, and other large corporations.

Roosevelt's boldest actions came in the area of conservation. During his years in the Dakota Territory, he had become increasingly concerned about preserving its great forests and its wildlife. As president he set aside some 194 million acres (78.5 million hectares) of public land as national forests, thereby making them off-limits to commercial exploitation of lumber, minerals,

and waterpower. In 1905 Congress created the Forest Service to oversee the national forests.

Several times during Roosevelt's first years in office, European powers threatened to intervene in Latin America. Roosevelt protested that such actions were a violation of the Monroe Doctrine, which President James Monroe first announced in 1823. This policy stated that the United States would not permit any European country to interfere in events on the two American continents. Roosevelt expanded the Monroe Doctrine to say that the United States would make sure that Latin American countries fulfilled their agreements with other countries. This policy statement became known as the Roosevelt Corollary to the Monroe Doctrine.

Roosevelt resorted to "big-stick" diplomacy most famously in 1903, when he helped Panama to secede from Colombia. Two weeks later the United States signed a treaty with Panama that gave the United States exclusive rights to build a canal across the Isthmus of Panama. Construction began at once on the Panama Canal. Roosevelt

his greatest accomplishment as president.

Roosevelt showed the soft-spoken, sophisticated side of his diplomacy in 1905, when he brought about a peace conference between Russia and Japan, which were then at war. For this service he was awarded the Nobel Peace prize.

LATER YEARS

After leaving office in 1909, Roosevelt embarked on a 10-month hunting trip in Africa and then toured Europe. On his return he was drawn back into politics. He believed that President William Howard Taft, his friend and hand-picked successor, had failed to carry on his policies and that he was needed to preserve the progressive movement. His friends urged him to be a candidate for president in 1912, but Taft defeated him for the Republican nomination. Roosevelt's followers then organized the Progressive party and nominated him for president. The party was nicknamed Bull Moose because Roosevelt, when asked how he felt, once replied that he

were soundly defeated by the Democrat Woodrow Wilson.

When World War I began in 1914, Roosevelt followed it with great interest. He soon decided that Wilson "had no policy whatever" and said so in a letter to the author Rudyard Kipling. He refused the Progressive party nomination for president in 1916 and supported the Republican nominee, but Wilson was reelected. After the United States entered the war his anger at Wilson boiled over when his offer to lead a division to France was rejected. By 1918 Roosevelt's support of the war and his harsh attacks on Wilson had made him the odds-on favorite for the 1920 Republican nomination. However, he died at Oyster Bay on Jan. 6, 1919.

CHAPTER 26

The only person to hold the highest offices in both the executive and judicial branches of the U.S. government was William Howard Taft. He was elected the 27th president of the United States in 1908 and later served as chief justice of the U.S. Supreme Court. Taft was well suited for these posts through his long years of experience. He had been in public office almost continuously since 1881.

EARLY LIFE AND POLITICAL CAREER

William Howard Taft was born on Sept. 15, 1857, into a wealthy and socially prominent family of Cincinnati, Ohio. He graduated second in his class at Yale University in 1878 and received a degree from the Cincinnati Law School in 1880. He practiced law very little, instead accepting a succession of political appointments—assistant prosecuting attorney (1881–82), collector of internal revenue (1882–83), judge of the Cincinnati

William Howard Taft. **Buyenlarge/Archive Photos/Getty Images**

Superior Court (1887–90), solicitor general of the United States (1890–92), and judge of the federal circuit court (1892–1900). By now he was dreaming of an appointment to the U.S. Supreme Court, his greatest ambition.

In 1900 President William McKinley made Taft chairman of the Second Philippine Commission. His task was to form a civil government in a country disrupted by the Spanish-American War of 1898. In 1901 he became the first civilian governor of the Philippines. He returned to Washington three years later to serve as secretary of war.

PRESIDENCY

As the presidential election of 1908 drew near, Roosevelt began to think of a successor who would continue his progressive reforms. He threw his support to Taft, who won the Republican nomination and easily defeated Democrat William Jennings Bryan in the general election. In 1909 he began a term that was doomed to trouble.

Unlike the dazzling Roosevelt, Taft was unable to popularize his accomplishments. Moreover, his administration was

overshadowed by quarrels within the Republican party. The party under Roosevelt was beginning to split into two factions. The conservative Stalwarts were popularly regarded as the champions of Wall Street and of the "money interests." At the opposite extreme were the younger Republicans, who wanted to go further than Roosevelt in the reform of big business and the trusts. They also called for more aggressive social legislation. Known as the Insurgents, they later became the Progressive party.

The first task before the new administration was a revision of the tariff. The West wanted lower rates; the East, with its manufacturing economy, wanted full protection. Nelson W. Aldrich, a Stalwart from Rhode Island and leader of the Senate, wrote the bill to suit himself, raising the duties on some 600 items. The Payne-Aldrich Tariff of 1909 was a victory for the Stalwarts. It seemed a clear violation of the party platform that had promised to revise the tariff downward. The Insurgents charged that Taft had abandoned Roosevelt's policies.

Conservation became a political issue soon after the tariff bill was enacted. Roosevelt had been an ardent supporter of the conservation of natural resources. Although Taft also backed conservation, his opponents charged that the new secretary of the interior, Richard A. Ballinger, was favoring the coal, mining, and timber interests that were exploiting the public lands of the West. A dispute involving Ballinger and Gifford Pinchot, the forester of the United States, became a scandal, forcing Taft to intervene. He upheld Ballinger, Pinchot's superior, and dismissed Pinchot. The Insurgents attacked Taft as an agent of big business and as a traitor to the cause of conservation.

In spite of these reverses, Taft's record as a progressive was as great as Roosevelt's. Twice as many suits were brought against trusts in his administration as in Roosevelt's. The 16th Amendment, authorizing a graduated federal income tax, was adopted.

Progressive Republicans made every effort to prevent Taft's renomination in 1912. They persuaded Roosevelt to run again as the candidate of the new Progressive party. The Democratic nominee was Woodrow Wilson. The split in the Republican party allowed the Democrats to win the election.

LATER YEARS

Soon after leaving the presidency Taft became a professor of constitutional law at Yale University. During World War I he promoted an international league to enforce peace, an idea endorsed by President Wilson. The League of Nations, established in 1919, owed much to Taft's support.

The last public service of the ex-president began in 1921 when President Warren G. Harding named him to the post he had longed for throughout his career—chief justice of the U.S. Supreme Court. Taft was happier in this position than he had been as president. He improved the Court's efficiency and helped bring about the Judiciary Act of 1925, which gave the Court more choice about which cases to hear. On Feb. 3, 1930, he resigned because of a heart ailment. He died in Washington on March 8.

The only candidate to run for the presidency of the United States from a prison cell, labor organizer Eugene V. Debs had been sentenced to prison for criticizing the government's prosecution of persons charged with violating the 1917 Espionage Act. It was the fifth time he had run for the presidency on the Socialist ticket.

Eugene Victor Debs was born in Terre Haute, Ind., on Nov. 5, 1855. He left home at 14 to work on the railroad and soon became interested in union activity. In 1875 he helped organize the Brotherhood of Locomotive Firemen. As president of the American Railway Union, he led a successful strike against the Great Northern Railway in 1894. Two months later he was jailed for half a year for his role in a strike against another railway company, the Chicago Pullman Palace Car Company.

Within a few years Debs had become a socialist and a founder of the Socialist Party of America. In 1905 Debs helped found the Industrial Workers of the World, but he soon quit the organization because of its radicalism.

Eugene V. Debs. **Library of Congress Prints and Photographs**

He was the Socialist party's presidential candidate in 1900, 1904, 1908, 1912, and 1920, when he received his highest popular vote—about 915,000. Debs was convicted of sedition, or encouraging opposition to the government, in 1918, and his U.S. citizenship was taken away. He was released from prison in 1921. He died in Elmhurst, Ill., on Oct. 20, 1926. His citizenship was restored 50 years after his death.

Novelist Theodore Dreiser was a leading American figure in the literary movement known as naturalism, which aimed to portray life in a realistic manner and depicted people as victims of blind forces and their own uncontrolled passions. Dreiser's first novel, *Sister Carrie*, was so shocking for its time that the publisher almost refused to publish it. The book was eventually published, but only in an altered form. Many of Dreiser's other novels sparked a similar response.

Dreiser was born in Terre Haute, Ind., on Aug. 27, 1871. He was the 12th of 13 children in a poor family. His formal education was meager, but he finished a year at Indiana University before beginning a career in journalism that led him to New York City in 1894. Supported by his prosperous composer brother Paul (who spelled his name Dresser), he wrote magazine articles. Distressed over the hostile reception of his *Sister Carrie*, he had a nervous breakdown. His next novel, *Jennie Gerhardt* (1911), was likewise condemned

Theodore Dreiser. Library of Congress, Washington, D.C.

because, like *Sister Carrie*, it was a story of unconventional sexual relationships.

Dreiser's next two novels, *The Financier* (1912) and *The Titan* (1914), were based on the exploits of the American transportation magnate Charles Tyson Yerkes. When these books were also unsuccessful, Dreiser turned from the novel to other forms of writing for the next 10 years. The publication of *An American Tragedy* (1925), based on a famous murder case, was his greatest critical and financial success. After this novel the quality and quantity of his work fell sharply. His last two novels, *The Bulwark* (1946) and *The Stoic* (1947), were published after his death. Dreiser died in Hollywood, Calif., on Dec. 28, 1945.

CHAPTER 29

UPTON SINCLAIR

Deeply committed to social justice, Upton Sinclair believed in the power of literature to improve the human condition. He wrote more than 90 novels but is best remembered for *The Jungle* (1906), in which he describes the wretched sanitary and working conditions in the Chicago meat-packing industry.

Upton Beall Sinclair was born on Sept. 20, 1878, in Baltimore, Md. He received a bachelor's degree from the City College of New York and did some graduate work at Columbia University. Sinclair published several unsuccessful novels before writing *The Jungle* for serialization in the socialist newspaper *Appeal to Reason*. Publication of the novel placed Sinclair in the ranks of the early 20th-century muckraking writers who used their pens to expose corruption and social injustice. Although it was intended to arouse sympathy for the conditions of the workers, the novel instead led to the passage of the first food inspection laws in the United States.

Upton Sinclair. Hulton Archive/Getty Images

Sinclair published numerous other protest novels, including *King Coal* (1917) and *The Profits of Religion* (1918). He also wrote 11 historical novels known as the Lanny Budd series. One of these novels, *Dragon's Teeth*, won the 1943 Pulitzer prize. Throughout his life Sinclair was a vocal supporter of socialism. He died in Bound Brook, N.J., on Nov. 25, 1968.

Ida M. Tarbell was an investigative journalist, lecturer, and chronicler of American industry. She is best known for her classic *The History of the Standard Oil Company*, published in 1904.

Ida Minerva Tarbell was born in Erie County, Pa., on Nov. 5, 1857. She was educated at Allegheny College in Meadville, Pa., and taught briefly before becoming an editor for the Chautauqua Literary and Scientific Circle in 1883. In 1891 she took her savings and went to Paris, where she enrolled in the Sorbonne and supported herself by writing articles for American magazines. S.S. McClure, founder of *McClure's Magazine*, hired her in 1894. *The History of the Standard Oil Company*, originally a serial that ran in *McClure's*, is one of the most thorough accounts of the rise of a business monopoly and its use of unfair practices. The articles also helped to define a growing trend to investigation, exposé, and crusading in liberal journals of the day, a technique that in 1906 President Theodore Roosevelt would label muckraking.

Ida M. Tarbell, 1904. Library of Congress, Washington, D.C.; neg. no. LC USZ 62 68572

Tarbell's association with *McClure's* lasted until 1906. She wrote for *American Magazine*, which she also co-owned and coedited, from 1906 to 1915, the year the magazine was sold. She lectured for a time on the Chautauqua circuit and wrote several popular biographies, including eight books on Abraham Lincoln. Later she served as a member of various government conferences and committees concerned with defense, industry, unemployment, and other issues. Her autobiography, *All in the Day's Work*, was published in 1939. She died on Jan. 6, 1944, in Bridgeport, Conn.

Russian-born international anarchist Emma Goldman conducted leftist activities in the United States from about 1890 to 1917. By the late 19th century she had given up her belief that violence was an acceptable means to achieve social changes and relied on organized speechmaking.

Goldman was born on June 27, 1869, in Kovno (now Kaunas), Lithuania, Russian Empire. She grew up in Lithuania, in Königsberg, East Prussia (now Kaliningrad, Russia), and in St. Petersburg. In 1885 she immigrated to the United States and settled in Rochester, N.Y. There, and later in New Haven, Conn., she worked in clothing factories and became acquainted with socialist and anarchist fellow workers. In 1889 Goldman moved to New York City, where she became friends with Russian anarchist Alexander Berkman. Three years later he was sent to jail for trying to assassinate U.S. capitalist Henry Clay Frick. The next year Goldman was jailed in New York City for causing a riot when a speech she delivered stirred up a group of unemployed workers.

When Goldman was released from jail in 1895, she began a series of lecture tours in Europe and the United States. In 1906 Berkman was freed, and he and Goldman resumed their joint activities. She founded the periodical *Mother Earth*, which she edited from 1906 to 1917, and wrote on anarchism, feminism, birth control, and other social problems.

Goldman opposed U.S. involvement in World War I, and she spoke out against military conscription, which led to a two-year prison sentence. Upon her release in 1919, she, Berkman, and other anarchists were deported to the Soviet Union. Her stay there was brief, and she spent the remainder of her life lecturing in various countries. Goldman died on May 14, 1940, in Toronto, Ont.

CHAPTER 32

MARGARET SANGER

The founder of the birth-control movement in the United States was Margaret Sanger, a nurse who worked among the poor on the Lower East Side of New York City. There she witnessed firsthand the results of uncontrolled fertility, self-induced abortions, and high rates of infant and maternal mortality.

Sanger was born Margaret Higgins in Corning, N.Y., on Sept. 14, 1883. She took her nurse's training at the White Plains Hospital and the Manhattan Eye and Ear Clinic. She married William Sanger in 1900. Although she later divorced him she kept the last name by which she had become well known, even after she remarried in 1922.

Sanger believed in a woman's right to plan the size of her family. In 1912 she gave up nursing to devote herself full time to the cause of birth control. In 1914 she founded the National Birth Control League and in that same year was indicted for sending out copies of the periodical *The Woman Rebel*, which advocated birth control. At that

Margaret Sanger. Time & Life Pictures/Getty Images

time the federal Comstock Law of 1873 classified such literature as obscene. Her case was dismissed in 1916. Later that year she opened the first birth-control clinic in the United States in Brooklyn, N.Y. She was arrested and served 20 days in jail in 1917 for creating a public nuisance. Continued government harassment brought public opinion to her side, and in 1936 the 1873 law was modified.

Sanger founded the American Birth Control League in 1921 and served as its president until 1928. That and later organizations became in 1942 the Planned Parenthood Federation of America. Sanger organized the first World Population Conference in Geneva, Switzerland, in 1927 and was also the first president of the International Planned Parenthood Federation, organized in 1953. She helped promote family planning in India and Japan. Sanger died in Tucson, Ariz., on Sept. 6, 1966.

CONCLUSION

When President Rutherford B. Hayes withdrew the last federal troops from the South in 1877, the wrenching Civil War and Reconstruction period of U.S. history came to a close. The new era would bring prosperity at home and newfound power abroad. Business titans such as John D. Rockefeller and Andrew Carnegie amassed huge fortunes as the country underwent an unprecedented industrial expansion.

Yet not everyone shared equally in the prosperity. Many of the immigrants who arrived seeking jobs and new homes struggled with abysmal working and living conditions in the cities. Attempts to improve their lot led Samuel Gompers and others to establish the labor movement. The abuses of capitalism and the oppression of minorities and the underclass also inspired a number of other prominent social reformers during this era. Jane Addams founded Hull House, one of the first social settlements in the United States. Ida B. Wells-Barnett and W.E.B. Du Bois sought justice for African Americans, while Susan B. Anthony and Margaret Sanger advocated for women's rights. The desire for social change also infused the work of journalists such as Ida M. Tarbell and Jacob Riis and novelists such as Upton Sinclair and Theodore Dreiser.

Social justice and other progressive ideas came to the forefront of politics with the Square Deal of President Theodore Roosevelt. In addition, his famous "big-stick" policy reflected another major development of the time — the emergence of the United States as a world power following the Spanish-American War. The country's ability to navigate world politics would soon be tested by the eruption of World War I in Europe, an event that would begin a new period of U.S. history.

abolitionist In U.S. history, a person who advocated for the end of slavery beginning in the late 18th century.

anarchism A doctrine stating that government is harmful and should be eliminated.

capitalism An economic system characterized by private ownership of the means of production (such as factories and offices) and in which market forces determine the way in which goods are produced and the means by which income and profit are distributed.

civil rights The nonpolitical rights of a citizen, especially the rights of personal liberty guaranteed to U.S. citizens by the 13th and 14th amendments to the Constitution and by acts of Congress.

conscription Compulsory enrollment of persons, especially for military service.

conservation Planned management of a natural resource to prevent exploitation, destruction, or neglect.

conservatism A right-of-center political philosophy that emphasizes the value of traditional institutions and practices and that prefers gradual rather than abrupt change.

Democratic party One of the two major political parties in the United States, the other being the Republican party. Historically, the Democratic party has supported organized labor, ethnic minorities, and progressive reform as well as greater government intervention in the economy.

dividend An individual share of company profits paid proportionally to stockholders, either in cash or in more shares.

honorary Given, elected, or awarded for outstanding service or distinguished achievements, rather than for the completion of formal educational or legal requirements.

humorist Somebody who writes or performs comic material.

industrialist An owner or controller of an industrial concern.

integrity Firm adherence to a code of especially moral or artistic values.

legislature A body of persons having the power to legislate; specifically an organized body having the authority to make laws for a political unit.

monopoly Exclusive ownership through legal privilege, command of supply, or concerted action.

Morse code Either of two codes consisting of variously spaced dots and dashes or long and short sounds used for transmitting messages by audible or visual signals.

muckrake To search out and publicly expose real or apparent misconduct of a prominent individual or business.

patent A writing securing for a term of years the exclusive right to make, use, or sell an invention.

philanthropist One who makes an active effort to promote human welfare; a person who practices philanthropy.

realism The theory or practice of fidelity in art and literature to nature or to real life and to accurate representation without idealization.

Republican party One of the two major political parties in the United States, the other being the Democratic party. Historically, the Republican party has supported minimal government interference in the economy, low taxes, and conservative social policies.

robber baron An American capitalist of the latter part of the 19th century who became wealthy through exploitation (as of natural resources, governmental influence, or low wage scales).

socialism An economic and political system that calls for collective or governmental ownership and administration of the means of production and distribution of goods.

stockholder An owner of corporate stock or shares of ownership in a company.

suffrage The right to vote, or the exercise of such right.

veto A power of one department or branch of a government to forbid or prohibit the carrying out of projects attempted by another department, especially a power vested in a chief executive to prevent the enactment of measures passed by a legislature.

Carnegie Foundation for the Advancement
   of Teaching
51 Vista Lane
Stanford, CA 94305
(650) 566-5100
Web site: http://www.carnegiefoundation.org
Founded by Andrew Carnegie in 1905,
   the Carnegie Foundation for the
   Advancement of Teaching is an inde-
   pendent policy and research center
   with the goal of improving teaching and
   learning.

Hearst Castle
750 Hearst Castle Road
San Simeon, CA 93452-9741
(805) 927-2030
Web site: http://www.hearstcastle.org
Once the home of William Randolph
   Hearst and now a museum, Hearst
   Castle is a sprawling estate featuring 165
   rooms; 127 acres of gardens, terraces,
   pools and walkways; and an extensive art
   collection.

Henry Ford Museum
20900 Oakwood Boulevard

Dearborn, MI 48124-5029

(313) 982-6220

Web site: www.thehenryford.org/museum

The Henry Ford Museum, a National
Historic Landmark, was named for its
founder, who used it to preserve some
of the most cherished symbols of the
Industrial Revolution.

Mark Twain Boyhood Home & Museum

120 North Main Street

Hannibal, MO 63401

(573) 221-9010

Web site: http://www.marktwainmuseum.org

The Mark Twain Boyhood Home & Museum
preserves the author's home as well
as those of his childhood friends who
inspired the characters of Huckleberry
Finn and Becky Thatcher.

Thomas Edison National Historical Park

211 Main Street

West Orange, NJ 07052-5612

(973) 736-0550 ext. 11

Web site: http://www.nps.gov/edis/index.htm

The Thomas Edison National Historical
Park preserves the estate of Thomas

Edison, including his residence and laboratory, where America's foremost inventor conducted his work.

WEB SITES

Due to the changing nature of Internet links, Rosen Educational Services has developed an online list of Web sites related to the subject of this book. This site is updated regularly. Please use this link to access the list:

www.rosenlinks.com/ioacb/newpowbio

BIBLIOGRAPHY

Benson, Sonia, and Stock, J.Y. *Development of the Industrial U.S.: Almanac* (Thomson/ Gale, 2006).

Collier, Christopher, and Collier, J.L. *The Rise of Industry: 1860–1900* (Benchmark, 2000).

Frost-Knappman, Elizabeth, and Cullen-DuPont, Kathryn. *Women's Suffrage in America,* updated ed. (Facts on File, 2005).

Greenwood, J.T. *The Gilded Age: A History in Documents* (Oxford Univ. Press, 2003).

Hakim, Joy. *Reconstructing America: 1865–1890,* 3rd ed., rev. (Oxford Univ. Press, 2005).

Hillstrom, Kevin. *Workers Unite!: The American Labor Movement* (Omnigraphics, 2011).

McCormick, A.L. *The Industrial Revolution in American History* (Enslow, 1998).

McNeese, Tim. *The New South and the Old West: 1866–1890* (Chelsea House, 2010).

McPherson, J.M. *Into the West: From Reconstruction to the Final Days of the American Frontier* (Atheneum, 2006).

Perry, E.I., and Smith, K.M. *The Gilded Age and Progressive Era: A Student Companion* (Oxford Univ. Press, 2006).

Sakolsky, Josh. *Critical Perspectives on the Industrial Revolution* (Rosen, 2005).

Schwartz, Eric. *Crossing the Seas: Americans Form an Empire, 1890–1899* (Mason Crest, 2005).

Woog, Adam. *The 1900s* (Lucent, 1999).